CHAKRAS

Explore Effective Methods For Restoring Equilibrium To Your Chakras And Enhancing Your Overall Health

(Comprehensive Health Manual On Achieving Optimal Chakra Balance And Promoting Chakra Healing)

Romeo Michaud

TABLE OF CONTENT

What Are Chakras? 1

Harmonizing And Employing Individual Chakras 3

Bringing Spiritual Energy Into Balance 24

Main Chakras 30

The Sacral Chakra For Establishing Connectivity 55

The Endocrine System, The Immune System, And Your Chakras 70

Yoga For Chakras 93

Changing The Chakra Energy Flow 101

Promoting The Restoration And Revitalization Of The Crown Chakra 127

What Are Chakras?

Denotative Significance The denotative significance of the term Chakra is derived from its literal meaning, which refers to a "wheel." This terminology is employed to delineate the energetic focal points within the human body, as these centers are perceived to be in a state of continuous rotation. Thus, the metaphorical depiction of a spinning wheel aptly encapsulates the essence of these centers. Elaboration: The chakra system adheres to a precise configuration whereby each of the chakra centers is aligned in a correct manner. These centers are designed to enable individuals to harness and employ the universal energy as a personal resource. If these centers are disrupted, the individual's personality is profoundly impacted at every developmental phase. One illustrative instance that aids in comprehending the concept of chakras pertains to the notion of electricity. In the event that a device is directly connected to the mains without allowing the adapter to modulate the voltage, an explosion may occur due to the excessive voltage surpassing the capacity of the internal system. In the realm of the human physique, the chakra centers assume a parallel function to that of the adapter in electronic devices. The chakras act as conduits that harness the omnipresent energy surrounding us, subsequently refining and disseminating it throughout the body. The lotus flower serves as the conventional emblem denoting the chakra centers. Every chakra rotates at a distinct velocity, and each chakra corresponds to a lotus that possesses a unique number of petals. Each of these centers is also accompanied by a corresponding numerical value.

Harmonizing And Employing Individual Chakras

People face various challenges when it comes to achieving equilibrium in the root chakra. For certain individuals, their attention is directed towards exceedingly fundamental facets, such as their dietary choices and bodily functions. Various cultural taboos may arise based on individuals' backgrounds, encompassing even the use of language deemed impolite in diverse social settings.

These societal prohibitions can pose challenges in accepting matters concerning both normal and abnormal gastrointestinal movements, as the performance of the digestive system significantly impacts various aspects of an individual's personal existence. These effects can vary from the need to strategize dietary arrangements to ensure elimination occurs during allotted rest intervals, to managing illnesses stemming from neglecting one's dietary needs.

The root chakra is additionally focused on fundamental requirements crucial to existence, which are nearly as vital as sustenance itself: habitation, suitable attire, and temperature regulation. These necessities necessitate the capacity to sustain oneself.

Acquire an image depicting the root chakra. There is a plethora of chakra coloring books obtainable from the market, alongside a diverse selection of line drawings accessible through the Internet. Allocate some time to meticulously fill in the coloring with the utilization of crayons, colored pencils, or markers.

Consider the components that are associated with this specific chakra. What positive developments are occurring in your life? Are you able to rely on regular, fundamental sustenance for each day? Must you structure your life in accordance with a specified work timetable? Are you in possession of a suitable accommodation to rest in during the night? Do you have concerns regarding the timely payment of rent, the uninterrupted provision of utilities, and ensuring an adequate budget for groceries? Alternatively, are you confident that these matters are under proper control?

Following that, contemplate the aspects that you wish to alter, components that would establish a more robust framework for your existence. Imagine the chakra illustration as a circular object that requires smooth and uninterrupted rotation.

Engage in the refinement of your mental visualization until you are able to perceive it revolving stationary just below the coccyx, functioning as a core foundation as well as a hub for the interconnected system of your entire chakra network.

Moving forward, we shall now discuss the sacral chakra. This establishment serves not only as a hub for physical activities, but also as a focal point for emotional well-being. Once more, this is a realm that is frequently influenced by cultural factors, encompassing suitable circumstances and individuals for engaging in sexual intercourse. There might exist a diverse range of matters with which to reconcile in this context.

This can encompass the act of embracing one's own sensuality, which is often suppressed in individuals during their formative years. It goes without saying that the emotions persist; however, they are suppressed or directed towards socially sanctioned actions like courtship and matrimony.

Given that the propagation of the species relies on the act of mating, it is customary in numerous societies to incorporate a ceremonial acknowledgment of a couple's declared commitment. This recognition holds particular significance as it frequently encompasses the desire to conceive and raise offspring. Nevertheless, unions can be established for alternative purposes as well.

Interpersonal connections that foster deep companionship, mutual comprehension, alleviation of solitude, and occasionally even guarantees of financial or physical protection are integral components of the relationships that evolve from this level. The sacral chakra is in close proximity to the root chakra. When one is neglected, the other subsequently endures adverse effects.

Once more, acquire a finely detailed illustration that depicts this particular chakra. Allocate a suitable amount of time to embellish it with hues, putting significant emphasis on your individualized sentiments pertaining to interpersonal connections at this magnitude. What aspects do you consider to be commendable in your interactions? Where are elements lacking? Once more, imagine the disk rotating slightly above the base chakra. Observe the ascending of the energy from the root chakra, traversing through the sacral chakra, both moving in perfect harmony.

Following that is the solar plexus chakra. The manipulative capacity over the innate impulses originating from the root and sacral chakras is derived from this particular chakra. This is the reason why a person of contemplation refrains from whistling at an aesthetically pleasing individual in public settings. Instead, they endeavor to establish a proper introduction or engage in conversation, provided that the person in question elicits admiration from the observer.

This is also the domain that determines whether or not the act of using the restroom can be postponed until a designated break period or if it would be appropriate to inform the supervisor about one's personal requirement to temporarily leave one's assigned area. It encompasses the capacity to refrain from finishing one's meal by delicately pushing away the plate, leaving behind the final morsel.

And it regulates the potential to elevate initial sexual attraction to a more profound stage where additional common interests, such as hobbies or backgrounds, can be avidly examined. Please proceed with the process of coloring, engaging in visualization, and directing your attention towards observing the rotation of the disks and the movement of energy.

Indeed, the solar plexus lies in close proximity to the heart chakra. Please locate and add color to a line drawing depicting the concept of this chakra. Observe how it absorbs the energies emanating from the three subordinate chakras.

This is the domain where hobbies and interests transform into fervent passions; where desire fused with affinity blossoms into profound affection; where modest commitments evolve into enduring lifelong alliances.

In summary, the heart chakra is responsible for perceiving and elevating fundamental emotions and requirements. Once more, observe this disk rotating with precision and gathering the energies emanating from its lower three counterparts.

Following that, we have the throat chakra. At this point in time, you have comprehended the established procedure. Obtain a sketch, craft a vivid illustration, concentrate on perceiving its rotational accuracy, and harness the energy derived from the preceding chakra.

At this juncture, the sentiments, dedication, and comprehension are effectively conveyed. Occasionally, this entails engaging in personal exchanges with your cherished individual or engaging in communication with the broader society. Please bear in mind that actions carry more weight than mere words; nonetheless, it is not coincidental that this particular chakra is positioned in close proximity to the vocal organs.

The frontal chakra, which has captivated the interests of intellectuals and spiritual practitioners for several generations, serves as an observatory for the world and its intricacies. Additionally, it possesses the ability to transcend worldly limits and perceive ethereal dimensions that are sensed rather than perceived through the conventional senses. For certain individuals, this phenomenon manifests as the ability to perceive auras, whereas for others, it manifests as an innate intuition that provides guidance such as the internal voice of caution and guidance. It harnesses the energetic potential derived from the lower chakras, metaphorically transforming it into something precious and invaluable. The equilibrium of this chakra holds significant importance, however, the pinnacle of its efficacy lies in the proper functioning of the lower chakras.

The energy emanating from the brow chakra ascends towards the crown chakra, akin to the ascent of fragrant incense smoke towards the divine entities. Once again, it would be beneficial to acquire a line drawing that can be filled with colors and utilized as an aid in directing attention towards this particular chakra.

As one's individual energy ascends, gradually pulled up from the soles of one's feet, likewise does the elevated energy - the unselfish dedication, the protective inclination, the sentiment of reverence and astonishment - descend through each of the diverse chakras, reverting back downwards through the soles of the feet into the earth, and ascending once more in an eternal cycle.

Therefore, the person who has successfully established a firm foundation and balance is consistently facilitating the circulation of that energy, from low to high and high to low, akin to a rechargeable battery operating on alternating current. Moreover, exhibiting an unceasing motion akin to that of a perpetual motion machine throughout the course of one's lifetime.

Chapter 4

The Third Chakra

The Manipura Chakra, alternatively referred to as the Solar Plexus Chakra, is sometimes acknowledged as the Fire Chakra. It is situated within the abdominal cavity, specifically positioned between the sternum and the navel, thus justifying its designation.

The Solar Plexus Chakra serves as the locus of power, representing the core of one's selfhood. The element of Agni or fire can be found in this location. Envision it as a bellows facilitating the circulation of air in and out of the fireplace. It's like breathing. The lungs undergo a process of expansion and contraction, alternatively regaining their original size, in sync with our breathing. The Chakra exerts influence on digestion and metabolism by energizing or stimulating these two processes.

This particular Chakra pertains to the realm of personal power or determined resolve. Whenever one determines to undertake a task, one promptly takes action to accomplish it. No dillydallying. By undertaking this action, you are effectively activating and harnessing your source of strength and authority. An individual who demonstrates self-assertion possesses a balanced and well-functioning Solar Plexus Chakra. That individual also exemplifies the ability to assume obligations and embrace challenges.

A harmonized Solar Plexus Chakra is manifested through a healthy sense of self-worth, continual personal development, embracing empowerment, exuding assurance, and displaying adeptness in assuming responsibility. On the other hand, an obstructed Manipura is evidenced by a state of passivity, elevated stress levels, and displays of emotional volatility. The flow of chakra is impeded by feelings of shame. It is imperative that you personally comprehend the aspects that bring you shame. Reflect upon the most significant letdowns you have experienced in your life. Reflect on each significant failure and any other sources of personal shame. Then, kindly consider embracing all of them without exception. Attaining equilibrium will remain elusive unless you acknowledge and accept this aspect of your existence. They have occurred, therefore it is prudent to acknowledge and embrace them. It is imperative that you cultivate the ability to embrace and cherish every facet of your being, including your imperfections.

Facilitate the awakening of Manipura chakra by engaging in yoga postures specifically designed to target this energetic center. The cobra pose, crocodile pose, and bow pose are a selection of yogic postures that may support the activation and stimulation of the Solar Plexus. Enhance your fitness routine by incorporating a balanced dietary plan consisting of fiber, intricate carbohydrates, and foods with a yellow hue (such as corn and yellow bell peppers).

During your meditative practice, visualize the hue of yellow. Consider the radiant luminosity emanating from the majestic, golden sun. Envision its presence within the depths of your very core. Envision the radiant golden light permeating your physical being, originating from the abdominal region.

Inhale deeply and engage in the repetitive recitation of the syllable "RAM." Regarding your affirmation, endeavor to affirm internally, stating, "I am aligned with the boundless power of the cosmos."

Root Chakra Healing

Should you ever find the necessity to assert your presence within the confines of this tangible realm, commence by addressing the restoration and balance of your root chakra. The subsequent methods prove to be efficacious for chakra healing:

Engaging in physical activities that target the muscles of the lower abdominal area, with specific emphasis on the muscles found in the feet.

Please press your feet firmly against the ground, as the objective is to cultivate a sense of grounding and establish a stable connection with the Earth. Engaging in this activity without footwear provides a heightened and profoundly fulfilling sensation, thereby facilitating the essential process of nurturing and restoring the root chakra. The act of facilitating healing in the root chakra involves engaging in predominantly physical endeavors, as the root chakra tends to possess the highest level of material solidity and significantly corresponds to the physical aspects of the body.

Practising Kundalini yoga

This method proves highly efficacious in enhancing, rejuvenating, and harmonizing the energy flow within your root chakra. This chakra is regarded as effective and efficient due to its focal point on the lower spine. Kundalini pertains to the vital life force associated with the Root chakra, enveloping the region at the bottom of the spinal column. The objective of this yoga practice is to alleviate tension in the lower spinal region and unlock the latent vitality contained therein. This particular style of yoga is primarily centered around seated postures and emphasizes the strengthening and toning of the abdominal muscles.

Eat Red Colored Foods

Nurture your base chakra by consuming crimson-hued nourishments such as apples and beetroots. Incorporating piquant seasonings such as red peppers and Tabasco sauce into your daily dietary regimen is recommended. Root vegetables such as carrots, parsnips, and potatoes, along with animal proteins like red meat and eggs, ought to be incorporated into one's dietary regimen.

Foods and fruits that are tinged with red, such as pomegranate, encompass the hue that symbolizes the essence of the root chakra, whilst vegetables that grow close to the earth evoke the energy of this chakra, which is deeply grounded. The process of protein digestion is prolonged and fundamental, therefore it is intricately connected to the functioning of this particular chakra.

Engage in the art and application of aromatherapy.

Indulge in experiencing various scents and observe your response to each aroma. Explore novel spices and fragrances within your immediate environment. Ensure periodic rotation of your fragrances, both in terms of perfumes and air fresheners. Scent-based therapies and curative practices prove effective due to the interconnection between this chakra and olfaction.

Use gemstones

Adorn your surroundings, including your premises and driveway, with gemstones, while also embellishing select rooms within your abode with these precious Earth formations. The gemstones that are advised for this particular kind of healing include garnet, smoky quartz, obsidian, black tourmaline. Please be aware that the planet Earth is one of the fundamental components of this chakra.

Bringing Spiritual Energy Into Balance

The Svadhishthana Chakra is located beneath our navel, and through its activation, we have the potential to transcend ignorance and attain heightened states of consciousness. As the passive spiritual energy inherent within the Root Chakra commences its circulation through the Sacral Chakra, gradual enhancement will be observed in our interpersonal connections. It necessitates a substantial amount of patience, discipline, self-restraint, and determination. However, diligent and persistent endeavors ultimately yield desirable outcomes. An increased libido is a prevalent occurrence when the innate vitality begins coursing through this particular chakra.

We are currently facing a diverse range of emotions. Our previous experiences of emotional distress, suffering, anguish, envy, letdowns, and similar sentiments. All aforementioned emotions such as joy, pride, confidence, passion, exhilaration, and so forth are fully expressed and laid bare. Amidst the tumultuous sentiments that permeate our thoughts and feelings, our fervent desire remains singular – to attain serenity. We acknowledge that all individuals, being human, possess a complexity that transcends simplistic categorization into purely good or bad. We have inadvertently absorbed diverse attributes during various time intervals, and this has occurred on a subliminal level, unbeknownst to us.

It is imperative that we acquire the skill to effectively manage these intense emotions that are currently overwhelming us. It is imperative to recognize that when we release or communicate our emotions to others, we are inadvertently nourishing the very sentiments we strive to overcome. We are also cognizant of the fact that suppressing these emotions will have an impact on our overall well-being.

Could you provide guidance on the appropriate method to regulate and manage these emotions?

Through the exercise of our intellectual acumen and acquired wisdom, we can eliminate them. By disengaging from our thoughts and emotions. By acknowledging that these thoughts and emotions are fleeting and maintaining our emotional resilience. Through the conscientious regulation of our thoughts and emotions.

Useful Practices:

The sacred syllable linked to the Svadhishthana Chakra is VAM. Through the concentrated attention on the vibrational essence prompted by this sacred mantra, we can harness the inherent energy within us to realign and restore equilibrium.

This chakra is commonly linked to the hue orange. Donning additional garments of this hue will enable us to regulate the influx of energy. Crystals such as Orange Calcite, Moonstone, and Coral Calcite will aid us in the process of healing and managing our emotions.

Throughout our contemplative sessions, we must endeavor to deliberately concentrate on our prior deeds and discern how they have influenced our current circumstances. Subsequently, we shall attain a comprehensive and impartial understanding and perception of matters. Once we adopt an unbiased perspective, we will develop the capacity to honor and value others, while concurrently cultivating an increased sense of self-assurance. This process commences internally, originating from our ability to display kindness and grant ourselves forgiveness. Embracing our vulnerabilities and acknowledging our previous errors will facilitate our healing process. Upon attaining self-awareness, we shall commence comprehension of our peers. When we cultivate self-love, we will embark on a journey of loving others.

Practicing postures such as Bhujangasana, Surya Namaskar, Mrigasana, and Dhanurasana facilitate the preservation of our equilibrium. The principles must be consistently applied on a daily basis throughout our lifetime, in order to attain a state of equanimity. Undoubtedly, the benefits justify the exertion.

Main Chakras

There exist seven primary Chakras, each of which possesses its unique designated color. Moreover, the Chakras symbolize distinct elements pertaining to one's physical, mental, and spiritual well-being. It is imperative to acquaint oneself with the constructive and adverse impacts that may be influenced by each principal Chakra locus.

Chakra 1 pertains to the color red and is associated with the Root area.

The progression of your chakras originates at the base and ascends towards the top. The foundational Chakra, located in the pelvic region, serves as the primary energy center and is ascribed to the hue of red. This serves as the foundation from which all of your physical energy originates. Maintaining the unobstructed state of this chakra, while facilitating the harmonious flow of energy through it, will afford the necessary stability to guarantee the optimal functioning of your physical capacities.

Every aspect pertaining to this Chakra is intricately connected to the innate human instinct for survival that is shared universally. It is integral to the maintenance of our physical and psychological well-being, promoting mindfulness and grounding of our mind and body.

The foundational Chakra serves as our connection to the physical realm and its energies, enabling us to gather vital life force from the Earth and transmit it harmoniously to the remaining six Chakra centers.

The primary responsibilities of this entity pertain to the adrenal gland, which plays a crucial role in the secretion and dispersion of hormonal substances. The stress-induced functioning of the adrenal gland exerts significant impact on our hormonal balance, thereby influencing our nervous system and subsequently activating the fight or flight response in us. By maintaining equilibrium and unobstructed flow in the root Chakra, one can contribute to the stabilization of the adrenal gland and its secretion of hormones.

The root additionally plays a crucial role in maintaining the well-being of the kidneys, prostate, bladder, and spine. If you are currently experiencing any physical ailments in these specific regions, it is possible that amending the energy flow in your root Chakra may provide some relief for at least a portion of these issues.

The blockage of the root Chakra gives rise to an imbalance in one's psychological condition, leading to manifestations of diminished self-worth, uncertainty, volatile conduct and thoughts, disturbances in sexual arousal and libido, challenges related to eating patterns, episodes of panic or anxiety, and elevated blood pressure. The intensity of the symptoms will be contingent upon the extent of the blockage and the degree to which the flow of energy is impeded.

Chakra two corresponds to the color orange and is known as the Sacral or Womb chakra.

The second point of focus for energy is known as the Sacral Chakra, positioned precisely in the region between the navel and the pelvis, in what is commonly referred to as the womb area. This particular energy centre is associated with the color orange. This particular Chakra is associated with various realms of sensual gratification. It is linked to your creative aptitude across a spectrum of domains, encompassing artistic talents and imaginative faculties. Additionally, it serves as the focal point for your sexual vitality and the physiological apparatus responsible for reproduction.

The passage of energy through this particular Chakra influences one's capacity to articulate joy, enthusiasm, and contentment, and it exercises control over the corporeal regions encompassing the legs, lower back, lower digestive organs, and the reproductive organs.

Your life force energy, known as prana, ascends from the Root Chakra and flows into the Sacral Chakra.

An obstruction of the Sacral chakra results in constraints on the capacity for imaginative and creative thinking, limitations on the enjoyment of pleasurable activities, and frequently diminished libido. Depression frequently emerges as a prevalent manifestation of obstruction or congestion in the Sacral Chakra, while addictive tendencies frequently demonstrate themselves as associated behaviors.

A obstructed Sacral chakra is also accountable for irrational cognition and behaviors, complications regarding procreation, atypical menstrual patterns, discomfort in the lower back and kidneys as well as urinary disorders, disruptions in digestion, and issues pertaining to gastrointestinal function.

Chakra three is associated with the color yellow and is referred to as the Solar Plexus.

The Solar Plexus Chakra is located at the abdominal region and is associated with the hue of yellow. This is the foundation upon which our sense of self is built. It encompasses various domains pertaining to our identity and the perception of our true essence. It exercises authority over all cognitive functionalities within this domain, encompassing our desires and the extent of our self-determination.

In terms of physical association, this Chakra is additionally interconnected with our gall bladder, liver, stomach, and pancreas, while simultaneously serving as our emotional connection to our essence. Due to its connection to our sense of self, apprehension is generated within this particular Chakra.

The unhindered transmission of energy within the Solar Plexus Chakra enables us to achieve equilibrium in our ability to regulate our cognition and subsequent behavior, thereby augmenting our self-assurance.

An obstructed Solar Plexus Chakra impairs our understanding of personal identity and engenders feelings of insecurity and unease. This phenomenon gives rise to a scrutiny of our thoughts as well as our behaviors, thereby prompting a necessity to exert dominance over others as a substitute for the relinquishment of personal control and self-confidence.

Insufficient lucidity, coupled with unpredictable thoughts, leads to the formation of plans that are seldom executed, thereby exacerbating the dearth of self-confidence being encountered. Elevated body weight and gastrointestinal disturbances are frequently accompanied by respiratory complications, as well as dysfunction of internal organs, neuralgia, and the presence of diabetes and gastric ulcers.

The fourth chakra is associated with the color green and is commonly referred to as the heart chakra.

The Heart Chakra is situated at the median point of the thoracic region and is associated with the hue of green. This particular Chakra is correlated with the realm of emotions, serving as the origin for sentiments like compassion, serenity, equanimity, and unbounded affection. This serves as the gateway to our inner being, facilitating a profound connection through which we can access and receive the divine wisdom emanating from our elevated consciousness.

This Chakra is accountable for the regulation and functioning of the circulatory system, cardiac muscle, thymus gland, pulmonary organs, thoracic region, dorsal region, and upper extremities.

Due to the emotional associations involved, an obstructed Heart Chakra may result in interpersonal disengagement, resulting in sensations of solitude and, contingent upon the extent of the blockage, an profound skepticism towards individuals previously regarded as trustworthy. Self-reflection intensifies and the tendency to pass judgment on others can swiftly develop into a pattern. Social anxiety is frequently encountered, leading individuals to seek solitude and withdraw from social interactions.

From a physiological standpoint, the consequences of an obstructed or hindered Heart Chakra may manifest as episodes of overwhelming fear or unease, impairments in the circulatory function, and hindered respiratory functioning.

Chakra 5 corresponds to the color blue and is located at the throat.

The fifth Chakra, also known as the Throat Chakra, is situated in the anatomical region of the neck and is associated with the hue of blue. It is ascribed to one's capacity to articulate oneself. This Chakra encompasses various facets, such as communication, acquisition and dissemination of knowledge, as well as principles of ethics and integrity. The Throat Chakra serves as the focal point for individual enlightenment and the acquisition of one's elevated essence.

This particular Chakra exercises dominion over the entirety of the throat and neck region, encompassing the various organs housed within and extending to the intricate network of nerves known as the pharyngeal nerve plexus. The olfactory organ, oral cavity, dentition and periodontal tissues, thyroidal gland, and pulmonary organs are likewise intricately interconnected with the Throat Chakra, alongside the upper extremities.

A Throat Chakra obstruction can present with indications such as inflamed throat, periodontal disease, oral ulcers, and inflammation of the larynx. Frequently, individuals commonly encounter an elevation in migraines coinciding with discomfort in the neck and even issues associated with the thyroid. It is widely acknowledged that in addition to these problems, individuals frequently encounter a range of issues related to an obstructed Heart Chakra.

From a societal perspective, an obstructed or congested Chakra in this region can give rise to significant issues. Social situations can prove to be challenging to navigate, while effectively articulating one's thoughts can present itself as a tangible matter of concern. Those in your vicinity may increasingly observe aberrant behavior on your part, as well as a growing tendency to withdraw from one's daily routines.

Chakra 6, known as the Indigo Chakra or the Third Eye Chakra located at the Brow.

The Third Eye Chakra, known as the Brow Chakra, is situated within the region between the eyebrows, precisely in the center of the forehead, and is associated with the hue of indigo. This serves as the foundation for our intuitive perception and spiritual insight/psychic faculties. Additionally, this is the juncture at which our artistic creativity is stimulated, and provided that the Sacral Chakra is unobstructed, this is where our imagination is granted unrestricted expression. The Third Eye Chakra serves as the portal by which we can attain entry into the realms of spirituality, enabling us to forge connections with every plane existing within the vast expanse of the universe.

This particular Chakra holds dominion over the pituitary gland, which exercises authority over the thyroid gland, the adrenal gland, and the hypothalamus, which regulates the functioning of the bodily organs. Additionally, it exerts a certain degree of impact on the well-being of the auditory organs, olfactory system, left ocular apparatus, inferior cerebral region, nervous system, and vertebral column.

Due to the significant sphere of influence governed by this Chakra, its physical impact extends to various crucial bodily systems while also effecting the spiritual energies of the remaining Chakras.

When obstructed, this Chakra can manifest extensive symptoms on physical, mental, and emotional dimensions. The prevalence of paranoid tendencies, coupled with symptoms of anxiety and depression, is frequently observed, and frequently coincides with the presence of delusional ideation, giving rise to behaviors that tend towards anti-sociality or unpredictability.

Migraines have the potential to occur frequently, leading to potential impairment of vision. There is also a potential for the development of sinus issues, as well as the manifestation of sciatica and seizures.

Chakra 7 – Violet (also known as ivory) - Crown

The Crown Chakra is positioned atop the cranium in close proximity to the pineal gland. This Chakra is associated with two hues and can be symbolized by either the color white or purple. This location provides us with the opportunity to fully delve into the core of our authentic being. When in a state of perfect equilibrium, this gateway can be unlocked, leading to the acquisition of knowledge that surpasses ordinary learning. Furthermore, it facilitates the attainment of a comprehensive understanding of our spiritual essence.

Furthermore, aside from the achievement of complete spiritual consciousness, this Chakra exercises control over the cerebral cortex and the pineal gland. All cognitive processes can be influenced by this energetic locus.

In the event that this Chakra encounters an obstruction, our capacity to establish a bond with others starts to manifest on a physical, mental, and emotional plane. We may experience a disconnection from our more elevated self, leading to a heightened sense of alienation and a perceived lack of belonging. Despite being in the company of loved ones, the sensation of solitude infiltrates our being, leading to a cognitive impediment wherein rational thought and future-oriented strategizing become formidable tasks.

Persistent sleeplessness and depressive symptoms manifest on a daily basis, accompanied by frequent experiences of delusions, intense headaches, and nerve-related discomfort. Moreover, our neurological functioning becomes noticeably impaired.

The Chakra occupying the fourth position (The Chakra associated with the Heart)

This particular chakra is rather self-evident, as it pertains to our capacity for affection and compassion. We have all encountered challenges within the realm of our chakras, hence it is quite conceivable that a significant proportion of us may be experiencing an impediment. When faced with obstacles, the free flow of energy is hindered, which can lead to the manifestation of physical or mental ailments within our bodies. A natural rhythm can be hindered by an obstruction, significantly impacting our encounters in life. If you have experienced emotional pain caused by a person you deeply care about, resulting in a sense of heartache, it is highly probable that this pertains to a chakra that requires personal focus and healing. The heart chakra allows us to experience love, inner peace, and a sense of joy.

In the event of an obstruction of this particular chakra, the adverse repercussions will manifest themselves in both our interpersonal connections and the tranquility we experience in our existence. If one experiences difficulty in forming emotional attachments or placing trust in others, it is often indicative of an ailment in the chakra system that necessitates healing and purification. It is crucial to bear in mind that our external reality is a manifestation of our internal reality. If one's heart is obstructed, the flow of love is impeded, resulting in a recurring sense of emptiness that permeates one's existence.

The fourth chakra serves as a spiritual center, facilitating the harmonious integration of the mind, body, and spirit. This energy serves to connect the foundational chakras associated with the physical realm to the higher spiritual chakras. Upon adequately addressing our physical chakras, our ability to heal our spiritual ones is significantly enhanced. The cardiac chakra symbolizes our interconnectedness with both individuals and the external environment. By arousing and stirring the energy of this spiritual center, individuals can cultivate compassion, forgiveness, and acceptance, thereby facilitating their embodiment in everyday existence.

In the event of an obstruction in this particular chakra, one may experience tendencies towards obsessiveness or withdrawal, stemming from apprehension regarding past traumas. To restore balance to this energy center, it is imperative to address and resolve lingering emotional wounds from the past. This entails embracing a process of forgiveness towards those who have caused hurt, recognizing their role as valuable lessons in our personal growth journey. Furthermore, it involves acknowledging that these experiences are an invaluable part of our life's intricate educational tapestry. In life, we are the sole creators of our own experiences, meaning that attributing blame to others serves only as a means of diverting our attention away from introspection. It is perpetually convenient to assign blame onto others. The greater the affection you possess, the greater the number of aspects in life that will emerge for you to cherish.

There is never a misstep in extending love. The elements comprising this chakra encompass cultivating self-compassion as well as compassion towards others, establishing meaningful connections with the world, and nurturing an all-encompassing love for all aspects, be they positive, negative, or morally ambiguous. The heart chakra, if disrupted, may lead to interpersonal difficulties and unhealthy dependency patterns. Continuously attending to the purification of your heart chakra proves to be a worthwhile endeavor, as it ensures the preservation of a harmonious equilibrium. The experience of deriving fulfillment from dwelling in a state of affection is unparalleled, for it aligns with the very purpose of our existence.

Ways of balancing

The anahata or heart chakra may be engaged and nurtured by practicing the yoga asana known as Camel Pose.

Additionally, engaging in activities such as intentionally closing your eyes and visualizing the Green hue enveloping your heart. Embrace the power of affection and direct your attention towards mending any wounds that may arise from previous experiences. Extending forgiveness to individuals from both your past and present. Visualizing them as individuals in their younger years within this realm can foster the capacity within oneself to cultivate sentiments of empathy and affection towards them. Commence the process of transcending any lingering feelings of anger or resentment, making room for love to permeate those emotional spaces.

Embracing forgiveness plays a significant role in relinquishing burdens and harmonizing the heart chakra. Various strategies exist to incorporate forgiveness into one's life, thus paving the path for love to permeate one's existence.

By retaining feelings of fear, hate, anger, and sadness, we are simply inflicting harm upon ourselves instead of accomplishing anything constructive. Acquiring the ability to fully embrace and appreciate oneself can serve as the initial stage in the process of restoring and balancing the heart's chakra. Engage in self-affirmation and trust your instincts when deciding on the subsequent course of action.

The Sacral Chakra For Establishing Connectivity.

The chakra that follows is referred to as the Sacral chakra. It has the responsibility of facilitating numerous crucial human functions. While the foundation of the chakra system lies within the root chakra, it can be asserted that this second chakra serves as its focal point. Accordingly, it oversees the process of life formation. Upon translation, its Sanskrit designation represents the abode of vitality. The Sacral chakra is situated in the pelvic region, specifically positioned beneath the navel. The hue commonly associated with the Sacral chakra is orange.

The second chakra enables us to ascend into our personal awareness. Upon the activation of this particular chakra, the process of nurturing and developing our individual identity commences. This provides us with an opportunity to acquire knowledge in establishing boundaries. We acquire an understanding and appreciation for maintaining personal boundaries through this process of learning. Due to our preoccupation with self-preservation, we develop a focus on what is known as relationship consciousness.

The Sacral chakra facilitates our personal growth and maturation. We acquire knowledge of the principles governing interpersonal dynamics. It facilitates our personal growth through the acquisition of knowledge regarding individual decisions and the recognition that these choices entail corresponding outcomes. It aids us in identifying the aspects we are prepared to forgo or negotiate in order to foster harmonious interpersonal connections.

As previously stated, this chakra functions as the focal point. It constitutes the essence of our sensuality, emotions, sexuality, creativity, and pleasure.

This particular Chakra assumes the role of facilitating the growth of our physical awareness. Located at our instinctual level, the Sacral chakra stimulates our primal urges in the realm of sexuality. Simultaneously, it alerts us to the possibility of looming risks. This is the method by which we engage with our emotional intuition.

The Advantages of Maintaining an Equilibrium in the Sacral Chakra

Individuals who possess equilibrium in their second chakra's energy exude no complications when it comes to the exchange and reciprocation of affection. These individuals are capable of harnessing their creative abilities and disseminating their innovative ideas. It is probable that they will develop and sustain wholesome relationships. They do not encounter any difficulties in regards to sexual and emotional intimacy.

Individuals who possess a harmoniously aligned Sacral chakra can rely upon their innate intuition when it comes to discerning others. They establish boundaries in a suitable fashion. They exhibit a sense of comfort and self-assuredness regarding their physical appearance. Furthermore, they possess the capacity to fully harness the inherent healing abilities concealed within a robust corporeal form.

Individuals who possess a harmoniously aligned sacral chakra exude an inherent sense of gentle warmth. They exhibit a pleasant demeanor while maintaining an appropriate level of social independence. Their friendliness is sincere.

An equilibrated second chakra enables one to exhibit an open and receptive demeanor toward the external environment. It provides one with both vitality and empathy. It can instill within you a sense of exuberance towards life. A well-harmonized sacral chakra engenders emotional equilibrium and facilitates a firmly rooted intuition.

The consequences of an overabundance of energy in the sacral chakra

Individuals who demonstrate an abundance of energy within their Sacral chakra may encounter challenges regarding the establishment and maintenance of appropriate personal boundaries. An illustration of this can be observed when individuals become excessively engrossed in a relationship, ultimately suffocating their partners. An excessively open sacral chakra can also result in an individual becoming highly receptive to emotions, developing a deep affinity with the emotional states of others, and assimilating them as their own.

These individuals display a propensity for being swayed by their emotions. Hence, they are prone to frequently experiencing intense episodes that drive them towards adopting belligerent and combative actions.

When one's Sacral chakra is excessively open, there is a propensity to internalize one's emotional state. This can potentially result in the onset of depression. You may exhibit a tendency to prolong your emotional attachment to grief beyond the expected duration. One might risk losing oneself by excessively contemplating individuals whom they have cherished and are no longer present in their lives. It could prove challenging for you to release and persist in harboring resentment towards individuals who may have treated you unjustly. Excessive sacral energy can engender an inclination towards possessiveness, extending beyond human relationships to encompass worldly belongings.

The manifestation of attachment and trust issues can be traced back to an impaired sacral chakra equilibrium. It can also result in feelings of sexual guilt. It has the potential to induce heightened sensitivity, timidity, and emotional volatility in individuals.

The implications of reduced energy levels within the sacral chakra

An abundance of energy in the sacral chakra leads to heightened emotional responsiveness. Conversely, a diminished vitality in the second chakra could contribute to a sensation of inertia or lack of zest. It has the potential to induce a sense of emotional detachment and aloofness. Consequently, it is possible for one to experience a disconnection from their emotions and a sense of detachment from their sexuality. Additionally, encountering obstacles in accessing creativity will be apparent. Your existence might resemble a monochromatic moving image. It demonstrates a lack of fervor and fails to evoke any profound emotions.

An asymmetrical Sacral chakra has the potential to manifest as sexual dysfunctions and eating disorders. It can also act as a hindrance to the establishment of a vibrational connection, which is of paramount importance in the process of attracting and sustaining relationships.

What are the factors that contribute to an incongruity in the sacral chakra?

The second Chakra is responsible for storing the recollections pertaining to our interpersonal connections. This encompasses both lessons pertaining to relationships and experiences of a sexual nature. The data contained within pertains to all of our associations, particularly those involving our familial connections. Negative encounters in interpersonal connections can have an impact on the equilibrium of the sacral chakra.

Traumatic incidents have the potential to induce a state of relational immobility. These distressing recollections are ensnared in a state of disarray and disconnection. As a result, it culminates in becoming trapped. Progress can only be achieved once the repercussions of these distressing occurrences are discharged and appropriately fused.

Guidelines for facilitating the restoration and harmonization of the Sacral Chakra.

The sacral chakra assumes utmost significance when it pertains to emotions, as it serves as the fundamental hub for emotional experiences. This also implies that the equilibrium of our sacral chakra is perpetually susceptible to disruption due to the experiences we encounter throughout our existence.

Nevertheless, the restoration and equilibrium of the sacral chakra can be achieved with minimal effort. It demonstrates a high level of accessibility, as it effectively facilitates the expression of one's creativity and emotions.

endeavor to place your hands atop your abdominal region. You might find it astonishing how consoling this can be. Why is it helpful? This is due to the fact that this particular area functions as the entrance to the realm of emotions.

Furthermore, incantations can also be beneficial in facilitating the healing of the Sacral chakra. A few instances consist of expressions such as, "I possess great affection and esteem for myself."

Hip-Opening Yoga

The tension we carry manifests in both our physical and emotional realms through our hips. Therefore, engaging in hip-opening yoga poses can be advantageous. Ideally, it is recommended to engage in a series of postures that specifically target the hip muscles in order to facilitate an expanded range of motion. Engaging in sustained body posture while directing focused attention towards achieving relaxation serves as a commendable starting point. A recommended yoga asana for opening the hips is the cow pose.

Engage in Dance and Pelvic Motion.

Engaging in rhythmic movement is an effective approach towards restoring equilibrium and promoting healing within the Sacral chakra. Adjust the positioning of your hips and feet. Relax and indulge in rhythmic movements to the melodic tunes that you most enjoy.

Tone Up

It is equally crucial for you to engage in exercises aimed at enhancing muscle tone and strength. It is incumbent upon you to nurture your physical well-being as a means of cultivating an optimal vessel for the spiritual self.

Several yoga asanas are suggested for muscular toning. These comprise the boat pose, yogic leg lifts, and pendant pose.

Imagine Orange

The sacral chakra is represented by the hue of orange. Envision the hue transforming into a radiant luminosity gradually embracing your lower abdominal region. Visualize the radiant orange light emanating from the lower abdominal region and directing its flow towards precise bodily zones associated with the accumulation of tension.

Devote attention to the remaining Chakras

The seven chakras are intricately linked together. Consequently, should there be an imbalance in one chakra, it is probable that the remaining chakras will also be impacted. Please bear in mind that the chakras function as an integrated system.

As an example, it is worth noting that the second chakra exhibits a strong correlation with the sacral chakra. Observe the impact of executing hip-opening yoga postures on the region of the throat. This is particularly accurate when practicing the fire log or the double pigeon pose. The bridge pose, conversely, is an exceptional exercise for simultaneously targeting the healing of more than two chakras. Effortlessly transition from one posture to another with an unhurried and graceful movement. Moreover, establish a correlation between the movement and the cadence of your breath.

Let Go

This exercise presents itself as a formidable challenge within this context. However, it is crucial to underscore the significance of relinquishing attachments to individuals, negative recollections, detrimental sentiments, and adverse occurrences. Do not hold onto them. This will merely contribute to an increased burden, which can exert a significant toll. As you acquire the ability to release attachments and let go, you will experience a reduced sense of burden and a heightened feeling of lightness, as you concurrently expand the space within your existence. In this manner, you embrace additional energy that will chart the course towards fresh opportunities.

In the course of one's existence, it is considerably effortless to encounter a multitude of obstacles. Consequently, you may discover that you become emotionally reticent. It also has the potential to foster an excessive reliance on others.

It might prove to be more challenging in practice than it appears in theory. However, it is imperative that you place trust in your intuition. Exercise restraint over your emotions, preventing them from exerting influence over you. All of these factors are vital components in the development of your optimal self, encompassing your highest level of physical and mental well-being.

The Endocrine System, The Immune System, And Your Chakras

What is the function and purpose of the endocrine system?

Hormones are synthesized by the glands situated within the human body, constituting what is commonly referred to as the endocrine system. Hormones are chemical substances that facilitate intercellular communication, ensuring the effective functioning of the human body. In the event of a malfunctioning endocrine system, individuals may encounter difficulties in managing stress, conceiving, or undergoing pubertal changes. Other individuals experience issues pertaining to their body weight, display indications of abnormally low bone density, and exhibit pronounced susceptibility to fatigue. On occasion, when there is a breakdown in hormone signaling, an excessive amount of glucose may accumulate in the bloodstream rather than being effectively stored in cells. This implies that you are experiencing a decreased level of vitality and are potentially developing an immunity towards insulin, ultimately resulting in the progression of type-2 diabetes. Due to these factors and numerous others, the maintenance of a robust and harmonious endocrine system is crucial for the preservation of your overall health and wellness.

The endocrine system comprises numerous distinct glands. The pineal gland, the pituitary gland, and the hypothalamus constitute the three principal glands located within the brain. Located in the vicinity of your neck, specifically, are your thyroid and parathyroid glands. The thymus gland is situated at the midpoint between the lungs. Your adrenal glands, which are diminutive in size, are positioned above your kidneys. The pancreas is situated posterior to the stomach. The location of your ovaries or testes, which are the final prominent pair of glands within your endocrine system, varies based on your gender and can be found in the pelvic region.

Hypothalamus
This gland maintains a line of communication with your pituitary gland. The principal purpose of this is to signal the pituitary gland to initiate or terminate the synthesis of hormones. Additionally, it serves as a link connecting your nervous system with your endocrine system.

Pituitary Gland
The pituitary gland serves as the principal gland of the endocrine system. It collects data from the cerebral regions and subsequently transmits instructions to various endocrine glands within the body, guiding them on necessary actions. In order to convey all of this information, it generates an array of hormones. One of the key hormones for which it bears responsibility is the growth hormone.

Additionally, it is imperative for females in the lactation stage to generate prolactin in order to facilitate the production of breast milk. Additionally, it plays a crucial role in the regulation of testosterone levels among males and estrogen levels among females through the synthesis of the hormone known as luteinizing hormone.

Pineal Gland

Once an individual is prepared to initiate sleep, the pineal gland within their body begins to secrete melatonin. This substance is utilized by the human body to initiate the process of relaxation and induce sleep.

Thyroid

The regulation of your metabolic processes is overseen by the thyroid gland. In the case of hypothyroidism, where there is a deficient production of hormones, the metabolic rates of the body experience a deceleration. Additionally, there is the potential for a decrease in your heart rate. In addition to decelerating your metabolism, the functioning of your gastrointestinal system retards, potentially leading to constipation and weight gain. In the case of hyperthyroidism, an excessive production of the hormone results in an accelerated rate of bodily functions. Your cardiac rhythm may accelerate, and you may experience rapid digestion leading to symptoms such as diarrhea and unintended weight loss.

Parathyroid
Located directly posterior to the thyroid gland are four smaller glands known as the parathyroid glands. They contribute to maintaining optimal bone health. This facility regulates the phosphorous and calcium levels in your body.

Thymus
During the developmental stages of childhood, it is of utmost importance for the thymus to function effectively. This gland is responsible for the production of T-cells or T-lymphocytes.

These cells are tasked with combatting infections and other intruders. It is responsible for the production of white blood cells. Following the onset of puberty, this gland initiates a process of gradual reduction in size, while retaining its indispensable role in maintaining the holistic well-being of the body.

Adrenal Glands
Numerous physiological processes, such as sexual functionality and metabolic regulation, are under the influence of the hormones secreted by these minute glands. The combination of the two results in the generation of corticosteroids. In addition, they generate epinephrine, otherwise known as adrenaline. This is the hormone that is released in situations of stress and imminent danger, commonly referred to as the "fight, flight, or freeze" response.

Pancreas

This gland serves the purpose of connecting two of the body's systems, similar to the hypothalamus. The pancreas serves as an important link between the endocrine system and the digestive system. This gland facilitates the body's recognition of the need to disintegrate food and retrieve essential nutrients from nutritional sources. Throughout this biological process, the human body synthesizes glucagon and insulin, two critical hormones that enable the adequate distribution of glucose into both the bloodstream and cells. Type 1 diabetes is characterized by the absence of insulin production in an individual. This indicates that the concentration of glucose in the bloodstream can reach perilously elevated levels. Individuals with Type 2 diabetes are capable of producing insulin, albeit usually at insufficient levels.

Ovaries
Progesterone and estrogen are a pair of hormones synthesized within the

ovaries, which are situated in the reproductive system of women. These two hormones play a crucial role in the development of breasts in women during puberty, maintenance of pregnancy, and regulation of menstrual cycles.

Testes
In general, males typically do not possess ovaries, while females typically do not possess testes. The testes of males secrete the hormone known as testosterone. This process is accountable for the synthesis of bodily and facial hair during the onset of adolescence. It facilitates spermatogenesis and also signals penile enlargement.

Health Issues Affecting the Endocrine System
As you age, the production of hormones through your endocrine system changes and may become more obvious to you. It is frequently observed that one's metabolism tends to decrease with the

progression of age. This phenomenon can result in an increase in body weight, even in the absence of any alterations to your dietary habits or physical activity levels. This can be attributed to the alterations in your hormonal balance with advancing age. Furthermore, this factor also contributes to an increased susceptibility to conditions such as coronary heart disease, type 2 diabetes, and osteoporosis.

Age alone is not the sole factor that can lead to alterations in your hormones and endocrine system. Age is inconsequential. The endocrine system can be affected by various factors such as stress, exposure to a specific chemical substance, and infection. Furthermore, genetic factors also contribute. Ultimately, one's lifestyle choices have the potential to impede the optimal functioning of the endocrine system and its related hormones. These extrinsic factors can contribute to the development of conditions such as early-onset osteoporosis, diabetes, and hypothyroidism.

What is the nature and functionality of your immune system?

A considerable number of individuals are aware of their immune system, however, only a minority possess a true understanding of its nature and operational mechanisms. It is imperative to grasp its significance in maintaining your overall well-being and adopt measures to ensure that your life remains in good health and harmonious equilibrium. When a foreign substance enters your organism, such as a pathogen or an infection, the principal function of your immune system is to identify and expel them. If it proves unattainable to expel them from your body, your immune system will proceed to eliminate and discard those cells on your behalf. For instance, upon exposure to the influenza virus, your immune system initiates a response. It appears to impede the viral settlement within your body, and in the event it is unsuccessful, initiates countermeasures to combat and prime your body for recuperation against the assailant. On occasion, it becomes imperative to employ medication in facilitating the recuperation or expediting the recovery process from particular infections and ailments. However, it is crucial to acknowledge that your immune system acts as both your primary safeguard and internal healthcare provider, aiding in your restoration following an intrusion.

A highly effective approach to bolstering this system is to mitigate levels of stress. When subjected to elevated levels of stress, the body's immune system is impeded from operating optimally or to its fullest potential. Consequently, it is apparent that amidst an especially demanding period or endeavor in a professional setting, one may observe a recurrence of common illnesses such as colds. However, during periods of decreased workloads or reduced responsibilities, individuals typically experience an improvement in their physical well-being. Your immune system is more responsive when you engage in leisurely activities. Hence, it is crucial for the sake of your holistic welfare to ascertain means of mitigating and regulating stress.

Amidst this period of tranquility, your immune system also ensures the preparedness of its reserve agents. This phenomenon is among the factors contributing to the characterization of your immune system as one of the most intricate physiological systems within your body, ranking second only to your nervous system, according to medical practitioners and scientists. It encompasses various organs, cells, and tissues that function collectively. Several of these "agents" comprise the bone marrow, gastrointestinal system, tonsils, integumentary system, lymph nodes, spleen, and mucosal tissues present in the genitalia, throat, and nasal passages. These sites serve the purpose of either housing the "reserve agents" or manufacturing them with the aim of promoting and maintaining bodily well-being. This is an incessantly operational system, devoid of rest or breaks. They serve as analogous to the "medical personnel in an emergency department" for your physiological well-being.

Over time, it gradually enhances your immunity, thereby bolstering your defense against specific diseases. Consider the plight of young children who continually endure a multitude of ailments such as otalgia and upper respiratory infections. As one is exposed to and combats such infections, their immune system undergoes the process of generating and storing specific defensive elements known as antibodies. These antibodies, in turn, enable the individual's immune system to effectively combat any recurrence of the infection. Vaccinations are formulated based on this model. They administer a minuscule quantity of the virus you wish to evade, effectively introducing it into your immune system. The virus is rendered attenuated or inactivated upon introduction, ensuring enhanced safety within your body, while still invoking the same response from your immune system. The human body only needs to generate and retain a sufficient quantity of antibodies, enabling it to effectively combat diseases such as meningitis, influenza, pertussis, and measles. Due to your past exposure or immunization to these diseases, when you encounter them in the course of your lifetime, your immune system can effectively combat them without causing you to fall ill.

Regrettably, with the advancement of age, there is a tendency for the immune system to experience a decline in its efficacy. With advancing age, individuals are increasingly susceptible to illnesses and medical conditions. This enhances the vulnerability to conditions such as different forms of cancer and arthritis. There exist additional factors apart from aging that can compromise your immune system, such as exposure to different chemicals or engaging in unfavorable lifestyle habits. However, there are also measures you can take in order to contribute to its welfare and enhance your overall well-being. "To illustrate this, you have the ability to:

Only consume alcohol moderately. For women, the recommended alcohol consumption limit is restricted to a maximum of one alcoholic beverage per day, while men should adhere to a maximum of two alcoholic beverages per day.

Do not smoke.

Maintain a healthy weight.

Maintain a consistent level of moderate to vigorous physical activity throughout your lifetime.

Make a selection of nutritious food options.

The Heart Chakra

The Heart Chakra is the fourth chakra out of the seven. This particular chakra is intricately linked with the hue of green and is precisely positioned at the precise midpoint of your thoracic region. Per your presumptions, its precise location coincides with the anatomical position of your heart. This particular chakra is commonly referred to as the "Cardiac Center" by certain individuals. The use of both terms seems to be interchangeable in various parts of the text pertaining to the concepts of energy healing and the energetic body. In this literary work, it shall be referred to as the Heart Chakra.
The Core Chakra plays a significant role in generating emotions of affection and empathy. When encountering a deficiency in the functionality of the Heart Chakra, individuals may encounter difficulties in experiencing emotions such as love or compassion towards the various aspects of their personal and external lives. One may encounter difficulty in personally encountering these emotions. Should

your Heart Chakra exhibit an excessive level of activity, it is possible that you may manifest an inclination towards unrestricted affection and compassion, potentially leading to behavior characterized by clinginess or excessive displays of fondness towards individuals. In the event that either of these situations is occurring, it is imperative to restore equilibrium to your Heart Chakra. You can achieve this by engaging in introspection and unraveling the underlying factors that contribute to your state of being. Often, we are affected by emotional experiences in our lives that cause us to be extremely cold or extremely affectionate towards others.

This chakra exhibits a direct correlation with the anatomical components including the heart organ, the lungs, and the thymus gland. If you are encountering distress in either of these matters, it may be beneficial for you to consider engaging in energy harmonization practices focused on your heart chakra, as a means to reinstate equilibrium and serenity within' them. Engaging in such actions may provide respite from any ailments that afflict you.

The Throat Chakra

As you might have surmised, the Throat Chakra, formally referred to as the fifth chakra, is situated in the anatomical region of the throat. The hue associated with this particular chakra is a luminous and spirited shade of blue. Generally, it is commonly observed as a pale blue hue, although it can be depicted in almost any variation of the color blue.

This particular chakra is attributed with the duty of facilitating sincere communication and facilitating the smooth expression of one's thoughts and feelings. In the event of an insufficiently active state of this chakra, individuals may encounter indications of social withdrawal, alongside emotions of frustration, sadness, or anger resulting from an inability to express one's true thoughts and feelings. Alternatively, in the event of excessive activity, there is a tendency to engage in abundant discourse while neglecting to exercise proper self-censorship, which may result in the perception of being authoritarian or discourteous. Alternatively, you could be characterized as a deficient listener, who listens solely with the intention of responding. It is imperative that when presented with either of these symptom clusters, one dedicates time to cultivating a practice of mindfulness, thereby granting oneself the ability to restore command over their vocal faculties. It is essential that you focus on cultivating a sense of honesty if you find yourself suppressing your true feelings, or alternatively, you should practice discretion or develop the ability to discern what information or opinions should be shared freely, as excessive disclosure may impede your personal growth and well-being.

The Throat Chakra is correlated with the respiratory system, thyroid, and all bodily organs linked to the region of the throat and oral cavity. Should you encounter any maladies related to these organs, it is plausible that you are manifesting physical manifestations of an imbalanced chakra. The prevailing symptom frequently cited is the sensation of having a mass or obstruction in the pharyngeal region. One can alleviate or mitigate these symptoms by reestablishing equilibrium in their throat chakra and expressing their authentic self without excessive verbosity.

The Chakra associated with the awareness and perception beyond the physical realm - The Third Eye Chakra

The position of the Third Eye Chakra is situated precisely in the area between and slightly elevated above the eyebrows. This particular chakra is characterized by the hue indigo and is widely acknowledged as the penultimate of the seven chakras. This particular chakra enjoys widespread recognition among many individuals, owing to its frequent mention in various texts and spiritual teachings.

The Third Eye Chakra is tasked with facilitating a profound connection to one's intuition, psychic perception, and profound discernment. When one is encountering a deficient functioning of their chakra, they may encounter difficulties in maintaining a connection with their intuitive faculties, or they might sense a disorientation and aimlessness in their journey through life. In a contrasting manner, in the event of excessive activity, individuals may experience heightened apprehension towards their intuitive perceptions and engage in excessive examination of mundane aspects of existence. In order to restore equilibrium to this chakra, it is advisable to engage in the practice of meditation. Your meditation practice can encompass the objective of inducing relaxation in the chakra, or alternatively, of expanding its accessibility based on whether it is exhibiting a state of insufficient or excessive activity. Consequently, it will facilitate your return to a state of well-being where you can recognize and heed your intuition without harboring any apprehension or undue suspicion towards the insights it provides.

From a physiological perspective, the Third Eye Chakra is closely linked with the pineal gland, pituitary gland, ocular organs, endocrine system, and cerebral functions. Should you find yourself encountering misalignment in this chakra, it is possible that you may manifest various afflictions related to either of these organs. One might potentially encounter headaches originating from the area behind the eyes or encounter disruptions in vision. It is plausible to experience regular headaches or cognitive dysfunction. Hormonal imbalances that impede overall wellness may arise, as well as abnormal functioning of the pineal and pituitary glands leading to either excessive or inadequate activity.

Restoring equilibrium to this chakra is likely to aid in the process of alleviating these ailments.

Yoga For Chakras

Below you will find a selection of yoga asanas that correspond to the seven chakras.

Yoga Asanas for the Muladhara Chakra

Kegel exercises - It should be noted that Kegel exercises are not, in fact, a form of yoga asana. It is in fact a form of stretching exercise that targets the muscles of the male anus and penis, as well as the muscles of the female anus and vagina. This is the pubococcygeus. It extends from the pubic bone to the coccyx. The Kegel exercise enhances its strength. It is highly recommended that you engage in this activity on a daily basis, maximizing the frequency as much as possible.

Shalabhasana, also referred to as the grasshopper or locust pose. This asana is highly beneficial for individuals experiencing renal issues. Hemoglobin is set to circulate along your lower extremities, ensuring optimal renal filtration to effectively eliminate toxic substances.

Janu Sirsasana - This yogic posture involves bringing the knees towards the head. It is a highly beneficial asana for individuals aiming to achieve weight loss. Employ the rhythmic breathing techniques in conjunction with stretching to effectively achieve optimal outcomes.

Yoga Asanas for the Svadhisthana Chakra

Bhujangasana, commonly known as the cobra pose, is an enduring yoga posture with a rich history. It enhances postural alignment, while fortifying the spine, in addition to augmenting flexibility. The practice of the cobra pose will result in enhanced circulation of blood throughout your spinal column. This has a positive impact on cardiovascular health as well.

Ardha Matsyendrasana is highly recommended for individuals seeking to enhance spinal flexibility. The twist pose, alternatively referred to as this, also facilitates enhanced circulation of blood to your nerves and vertebrae. Additionally, this will enhance the functioning of vital organs, including the spleen, pancreas, and liver. Hatha Yoga Pradipika has recommended its practice.

Ardha Pada Hastasana is an effective posture for enhancing the fortitude of the lower limbs, quadriceps, abdominal musculature, as well as the various muscles encompassing the glutes and pelvic region. The alleviation of hip stiffness is possible. Additionally, this treatment will effectively eliminate the surplus adipose tissue from your gluteal region and lower extremities.

Yoga Asanas for the Manipura Chakra

Dhanurasana, or commonly referred to as the bow pose, is considered one of the most beneficial asanas, irrespective of one's aspirations. It provides benefits to various physiological regions of your body. This practice has been highly recommended by the Hatha Yoga Pradipika.

Vajroli Mudra – This posture is specifically intended to target the functions of your urinary and reproductive systems. It will effectively enhance the strength and conditioning of your entire abdominal region.

Nakra-Kriyas is an excellent posture for individuals with compromised spinal health. Referred to as the crocodile pose, in this posture, there exists a constant state of motion as one remains in motion throughout. This can be accomplished in a seated, upright, or reclined position. If assuming a reclining position, it is recommended to maintain a posture in which both knees remain flexed while keeping the feet positioned beneath the thighs.

Yoga Asanas for the Activation of Anahata Chakra

Ustrasana, also known as the camel pose, is designed to elongate the muscles of the arms, back, hips, and thighs. This will facilitate the expansion of your chest and promote the elongation of your lower back. Maintain a slight backwards tilt of your head while ensuring that it remains in a state of utmost relaxation.

Matsyasana, commonly referred to as the fish pose, involves a complete stretching of the spinal column. Your thoracic region is going to experience an enlargement. Furthermore, there will be an extension of the muscles in your throat and neck. Consequently, this will consequently lead to the expansion of your entire cardiac region. This particular posture has been endorsed by the Hatha Yoga Pradipika.

Sukh-Purvak – This technique entails controlled breathing. This is an immensely potent technique for accessing and activating your chakra centers.

Yoga Asanas for the Vishuddha Chakra

Halasana, commonly referred to as the plough pose, offers a beneficial spinal stretch. Additionally, it facilitates the circulation of blood to the throat.

Sarvangasana, classified as a posture within the Shoulder Stand group, presents diverse modifications.

Yoga Asanas for the Ajna and Sahasrara Energy Centers

Matsyasana allows for complete extension of the back, facilitating a thorough stretch in the fish pose. Your chest gets expanded. The throat and neck are extended. This will facilitate accessibility to the entire cardiac region.

Yoga Mudra – This represents the posture of sealing or closure. Apply pressure to the heel against the yoni area while concurrently bringing the head downwards towards the chin. Exhale slowly. Commence inhalation through the left nostril in the first instance, followed by the right nostril. It will offer alleviation from symptoms of indigestion and colic.

Changing The Chakra Energy Flow

As chakras are profoundly receptive to energy and influenced by one's lifestyle and mindset, the methods used to purify and restore balance to your chakras will invariably consist of aspects that you consciously recognize but potentially overlook or excessively engage in. Several of the alternative proposals may be recognized, deriving from various other sources. This implies that you may encounter fewer adjustments that need to be made in order to facilitate the healing and purification of your chakras. Demonstrating these straightforward methodologies will serve as an adequate initiation towards achieving purified and revitalized chakras.

Nevertheless, there might arise occasions when a situation appears to be immovable, and none of the aforementioned recommendations appear to be effective. It is advisable to consider engaging the services of a professional consultant who can assist in rectifying the disruptions in the energy flow to restore it to its optimal state. In these instances, the professionals in question will encompass shiatsu massages, Reiki, and other modalities that facilitate the harmonious circulation of vital energy. If you are not acquainted with anyone employed in these fields, contacting a reputable martial arts institution could potentially yield recommendations, or consulting a dependable chiropractor might provide insights regarding suitable individuals. The utilization of chakras in conjunction with therapy and other contemplated techniques can lend support in addressing profound fears and obstacles.

You can tangibly perceive the efficacy of this practice! The act of imbuing positive energy or harmonizing excessively active chakras will heighten your self-assurance, across various domains of your life. The depletion of pessimistic energy will be significantly reduced, and you will not experience fatigue from mere social interactions.

In order to restore equilibrium to the chakras, it is imperative to concentrate on the distinct areas of expertise associated with each. This exercise provides the opportunity for the addition of positive energy to every chakra, ultimately facilitating the process of healing for those that require it. Your personal reflections and sentiment shall serve as the most reliable compass in identifying underactive and overactive chakras, thereby determining the aspects to be abstained from or incorporated into your daily regimen.

Healing the Chakras

This exercise will commence once more at the foundational root chakra, and proceed gradually upwards. Implementing the proposed recommendation will enhance the vitality of the chakra, while neglecting to do so will diminish the energy residing within that specific region. Chakras that are imbalanced will remain motionless or rotate in the opposite direction, while overly stimulated chakras will become a turbulent vortex of energy. Your objective is to achieve a consistent and continuous clockwise circulation.

Root

The root chakra ought to possess a distinct crimson hue, and one should exhibit minimal trepidation regarding matters of survival. The factors that will contribute to the bolstering of these chakras are:

Incorporating crimson items such as strawberries, tomatoes, and hot peppers into your diet can augment the piquancy of your culinary experiences.

Devise a financial plan and explore means of further economizing.

If weather conditions permit, it is advisable to dedicate time to being barefoot; however, any kind of physical activity significantly nurtures this energy center.

The assistance of warm fragrances and various red gemstones aid in reinforcing this idea.

Sacral

The second chakra is the repository for entrenched beliefs and remorseful emotions. To reinforce the activation of this chakra, consider:

Consuming orange-colored items such as carrots, oranges, and peppers.

Devote a portion of your day to engaging in an activity that brings you joy.

Indulge in observing or perusing a tale of romance.

Taking a bath solely for the purpose of relaxation can aid in the enhancement of the energy flow within this particular chakra.

Fragrances of romance, as well as moonstones and gemstones in shades of orange, can also aid in achieving the desired effect.

Solar Plexus

As the final of the lower chakras, it represents the manifestation of self-assurance and mastery that we exhibit in our daily existence. The most effective means of providing support for this are:

Consuming yellow-colored food items such as corn, lemon, and certain varieties of peppers.

In addition to the yellow stones, lemon provides a delightful aroma.

Take caution to refrain from engaging in negative self-talk or criticisms pertaining to your own abilities or the quality of your work. Instead, prioritize surrounding yourself with individuals who provide you with support and encouragement.

When experiencing stress, partake in the consumption of a soothing herbal infusion. Chamomile is a preferred choice of mine.

Heart

Acquiring the skill of self-care can be challenging, particularly if it has been neglected over a significant period of time. Take time to:

Make arrangements to engage in activities that bring you joy, and ensure that you adhere to your commitment without fail.

Engage in active listening, as opposed to passively hearing: one should initially apply this principle with acquaintances

Consume leafy greens and indulge in a nutritious green smoothie to promote cardiovascular health.

This chakra serves as a unifying force, harmonizing the lower and upper chakras, thus requiring the use of rose and green colors and stones to provide optimal support for its equilibrium.

Throat

Verbal expression conveys our vibrancy and serves as the most effective means to impart the energy of this chakra. The most superior ideas consist of:

Visualize an individual with whom you typically experience discomfort conversing, and envision yourself engaging in a relaxed dialogue with them.

Please bear in mind that a politely yet firmly uttered "No" carries complete meaning on its own. You are required to provide explanations on a limited number of occasions.

Maintain confidentiality, while being predominantly transparent and truthful in your interactions with others.

The fragrance emanated by flowers within the blue and purple spectrum, along with the azure hue of stones, shall contribute to the reinforcement of your chakra.

Third Eye

The ability to ascertain one's own thoughts is a skill that has been postulated by philosophers dating back to the period of ancient Greece and Rome, and conceivably even predating that era. Enhancing one's perspective by gaining a broader understanding of the world, as well as one's own position within it, can be achieved through:

Deeply pigmented edibles such as blackberries and pomegranates, alongside minerals in shades of profound blue

Pay close attention to discussions in order to identify subtle nuances that could provide valuable insight into individuals who would otherwise be difficult to comprehend.

If you possess an intuition, and it proves to be accurate, derive pleasure from it!

Take heed of individuals whom you perceive as either positive or negative, and ascertain whether your intuitive impressions align with subsequent experiences.

The fragrances and flavors of the more profound spices (such as basil and rosemary) appear to evoke the energy of this chakra.

And finally,

Crown

As previously mentioned, the coronet shall manifest any disarray within the lower chakras. This chakra embodies the highest level of spirituality, indicating our inherent bond with the Divine. "In order to receive optimal assistance, this chakra exhibits optimal responsiveness to:

The light purple and white stones, along with traditional aromas of frankincense

Daily moments of tranquility, ideally through the practice of meditation and prayer,

Seek something that brings joy and allows yourself to indulge in it.

Pay heed to your transcendent linkage: you may be prompted to embark upon something novel.

This will initiate the process of restoring and purifying your chakras. There are alternative measures that you can undertake to assist them in achieving a state of equilibrium. These are activities that you are capable of engaging in, however, they require a heightened level of attention in order to effectively harmonize your energies.

The practice of meditation, encompassing its various modalities, presents an excellent opportunity to leverage the newly acquired energies in order to harmonize and restore equilibrium to your chakras. The eventual acquisition of insights will guide you towards a path that aligns strongly with your best interests.

Strolling through natural surroundings, or engaging in the practice of yoga, has long been acknowledged for its inherent ability to foster harmony between the body and the mind. Engaging in a leisurely stroll alongside a companion can significantly contribute to the enhancement of one's listening skills, self-care practices, demonstration of compassion, and elevation of mental and emotional well-being.

Taking time to take care of yourself, and do the things that you love, or have always wanted to do will liberate you from set-in habits and thought patterns. Even in the event of an unsuccessful transition to a new career, engaging in a new hobby or reigniting an old one will effectively disrupt your established routine.

Taking a moment to partake in a serene atmosphere, detached from the chaotic clamor and technological noises of contemporary society, will facilitate a state of relaxation and serve as a means to allow the harmonious energies of the chakras to flow freely. If you have a preference for minimizing time spent apart, consider arriving at your appointment a couple of minutes ahead of schedule and allowing yourself to unwind in a designated waiting area or at a suitable sitting area until your appointment commences. Alternatively, if your schedule permits, arrange an appointment at a spa and indulge in a luxuriant experience of pampering and relaxation.

Incorporate these fundamental elements into your daily routine and enjoy the advantages that result. According to the principles of the Laws of Attraction, redirecting your focus slightly can result in a shift in attention towards alternative emotions and energies.

Chapter 3: Determining the Presence of Chakra Imbalances

There are instances wherein you might have experienced the impact on both your physical and mental well-being. This is due to the presence of imbalances in your chakras. With the inclusion of this section, you will acquire comprehensive insight into the manner in which your physiological response might manifest in the event of an imbalance in the vital energy centers, known as chakras, within your corporeal frame. One will come to observe that the occurrence of an imbalance in even a single chakra elicits a varied array of responses.

Root Chakra

An earlier reference states that the root chakra is situated at the lowermost part of the spine, in proximity to the coccyx. When one's root chakra is unbalanced, the negative consequences will be felt extensively.

One will notice a severe affliction to the lower extremities, namely the legs and feet, in the presence of an imbalance in this particular chakra. Additionally, it can be observed that your immune system experiences significant detriment. This particular chakra tends to inflict greater detriment upon males in the event of an imbalance within the energetic system. It is possible that an imbalance in this chakra may lead to the manifestation of constipation.

This specific chakra primarily pertains to the hyperactivity of your adrenal glands, thereby influencing your physiological response to potential danger, commonly referred to as the fight or flight response. In the event of an imbalance in this chakra, you may experience heightened emotional states and notice a decrease in the efficacy of your reactions. You will encounter a pressing urgency to seek refuge and sustenance.

Sacral Chakra

This represents a chakra that consistently governs one's emotional state and capacity for love. Should an imbalance occur within this chakra, one would undoubtedly observe discernible alterations in their behavioral patterns.

You will discover that your reproductive system has undergone significant disturbance due to an imbalance in this chakra. You will observe that the imbalance in this chakra has had an impact on both your hips and lower back. You may experience severe discomfort and given the proximity of your kidneys to your reproductive system, it is possible that you may encounter issues with renal function, as well as other urinary disturbances.

You will discover that you have hindered your ability to experience any emotions regarding your loved ones. You will observe that you maintain emotional distance and encounter challenges in articulating your sentiments to others. You will inevitably experience a growing trepidation towards emotions, leading to a persistent state of depression.

Solar Plexus Chakra

This particular chakra is intricately associated with your creative faculties, and any disharmony within it may manifest as specific physiological issues. You may experience sensations of fatigue or diminished energy levels, regardless of your level of activity during the day. You may likely experience significant levels of stress as well. Your digestive system may also experience some degree of stress. Additionally, it is possible that you may be experiencing ulcers, a condition that can contribute to more severe complications.

Additionally, you might experience emotional imbalances that could contribute to a decreased sense of self-assurance. As a result of this, your self-confidence will diminish as you start to scrutinize each decision you make in your life. One may commence engaging in self-criticism and potentially develop aversion towards their physical appearance and behavior.

Heart Chakra

As previously stated, this chakra resides in the central region of your chest, in close proximity to your heart. When an inequilibrium arises within this particular chakra, it becomes evident that both the respiratory and cardiovascular systems experience profound disturbances. Individuals may discover a heightened predisposition to cardiovascular ailments, potentially experiencing instances of stroke on more than one occasion. You will find yourself having issues with asthma, bronchitis or even wheezing.

In the event of an asymmetry within this chakra, it is conceivable that one might develop an excessive preoccupation with another individual. One will discover themselves developing an intense fondness for that individual, reaching a point where it becomes an insatiable desire. If the individual in question is deceased, you may possibly experience a scenario in which you have no desire to continue living. There is a high likelihood that you will experience feelings of insecurity within the relationship, leading to frequent questioning regarding the whereabouts of your partner. Additionally, you might also experience intense envy and occasional outbursts of anger.

Throat Chakra

This particular chakra is situated in close proximity to the throat region and it consistently influences the surrounding regions of the throat when it attains equilibrium. You might start experiencing complications with your vocal cords and occasionally encounter challenges related to your thyroid gland. It is possible that you may experience certain discrepancies in the production of this hormone. There might be occasions when you experience discomfort in your vocal cords, resulting in significant challenges in verbal communication.

In the event of an imbalance in this particular chakra, one may potentially encounter difficulties in engaging in effective interpersonal communication due to a lack of self-assurance and subsequent hesitancy in interacting with others. Additionally, you may also encounter a situation where communication about personal matters or any subject becomes unattainable. One might also inquire about the ethical implications of their actions and contemplate the moral appropriateness of their choices.

Third Eye chakra

Located precisely between the ocular region, this chakra's disharmony adversely impacts visual acuity. You may experience visual impairment and develop an enduring headache that hinders your ability to remain calm. The proximity of your ears to your eyes makes it possible for any affliction affecting your eyes to potentially impact your ears as well. You may discover that your auditory capacity has been significantly impaired.

You will discover that you possess certain discrepancies in managing your emotions as well. On certain occasions, one might experience fluctuations in mood due to uncertainty regarding one's emotional state. One might gradually lose awareness of their own weaknesses and consequently become inclined to identify and highlight the flaws of others. You may increasingly lose sight of your duties and opt to indulge in idle reverie.

Crown Chakra

It has been conveyed to you that this chakra can be located at the cranial region, specifically situated at the vertex of your cranium. In the event of disruptions in this chakra, one may experience a multitude of psychological ailments. It is conceivable that you may encounter instances of enduring depression. As you continue to work or study, you will experience a gradual increase in the challenge to sustain focus. You may discover that you become highly attuned to your surroundings and unfavorable towards any alterations that have been introduced to your environment.

It is also advisable to commence self-reflection and diligently scrutinize your actions at each juncture. Furthermore, you might experience concerns and contemplations regarding the individuals in your immediate vicinity, causing you to question your own worth and ponder the legitimacy of your position within society. Although you may possess exceptional proficiency in your role, it is possible for doubts to arise regarding the suitability of your profession.

You will discover that certain characteristics, which have been previously stated, also resonate within your own self. This does not signify that one is incapable of self-healing. The subsequent chapters will provide you with the means to effectively restore your well-being. You shall acquire knowledge regarding the harmonization of energy within the chakras.

Promoting The Restoration And Revitalization Of The Crown Chakra

The term 'sahasrara' in Sanskrit is used to denote the seventh chakra, commonly known as the 'crown chakra'. Its placement is situated atop one's cranial region, possessing the hue 'violet', and connoting the essence of 'intellectual contemplation'. Its corresponding symbol is depicted as presented underneath.

What is the Function of the Crown Chakra?
The crown chakra is alternatively referred to as the 'chakra of a thousand petals' due to the belief that its opening allows for the attainment of comprehensive wisdom and a profound spiritual connection with one's own essence. It represents the highest energetic center among all chakras and governs the capacity to experience enthusiasm, establish a profound

connection with one's true essence, transcend superficial perceptions, foster fervor, and attain a state of ultimate enlightenment. Additionally, it governs the processes of your brain and addresses issues pertaining to your cognitive ability.

What are the Consequences of an Obstructed Crown Chakra versus an Activated Crown Chakra?

When the crown chakra becomes unblocked, an individual experiences a profound sense of self-connection, displays wisdom and intuition, exhibits self-mastery, engages in profound introspection, and cultivates a heightened state of mindfulness and awakened consciousness.

Nevertheless, in the event of its obstruction, one may encounter feelings of skepticism, indifference, a disconnection from one's spiritual essence, inclinations towards self-destructive behavior, excessive sleep, a lack of inspiration or motivation, a state of bewilderment concerning life's direction, overwhelming exhaustion, and pronounced symptoms of depression. The subsequent remedies serve as an excellent means to reinstate equilibrium to the ailment.

Methods for Restoring Balance to the Crown Chakra

The subsequent actions, if consistently implemented, contribute to the restoration of your crown chakra.

Crystal Healing

Adorn yourself with gemstones such as Sugilite, Clear Quartz, and Selenite in the shape of a pendant or bracelet, as their transparent and revitalizing energy harmonizes your crown chakra. Furthermore, it is advised to grasp the selected stone for a period of 10 minutes each day while envisioning an activation of your crown chakra.

Meditative Practice

Please relax and engage in deep breathing exercises. Please, shut your eyes and visualize a lotus of violet hue blossoming atop your cranium. Imagine its growth in size and radiant violet luminescence encompassing your entire being.

Partake in this ritual for a duration of 10 to 20 minutes each day in order to facilitate the healing and activation of your crown chakra.

Eat Right

Incorporating violet foods such as eggplant and passion fruit, as well as herbal teas like ginger and peppermint tea, can have a profound effect on balancing and aligning your crown chakra. As a result, I highly recommend integrating these nourishing elements into your daily dietary regimen.

Affirmations

Furthermore, it is advisable to recite any of the subsequent affirmations or their related counterparts on a daily basis.

I am entirely receptive to the reception of spiritual or divine guidance.

I maintain a strong connection with my spiritual essence.

I am in harmony with the cosmos.

I possess illuminating qualities and emit luminosity.

It is imperative that you engage in diligent practice of these exercises while maintaining a steadfast conviction in their efficacy, in order to fully realize their potential benefits.

The sixth chakra is referred to as Ajna, commonly recognized as the chakra associated with the third eye. The term "Ajna" originates from the Sanskrit language with a translation implying an essence surpassing conventional wisdom. The third eye is responsible for perceiving and comprehending not the visual stimuli of the material world, but rather the spiritual insights communicated from the metaphysical plane. Organically and in accordance with its given designation, this chakra is located on the frontal region of your head, situated above the horizontal line of your eyebrows and between your eyes. The hypothalamus is intricately linked to both the pituitary gland and the brain, serving as the focal point of intuitive perception within the human body.

From this perspective, it can be noted that the third eye chakra serves as a conduit to the sixth sense, enabling one to perceive the spiritual realm and possess the capacity to direct their consciousness and thoughts towards this dimension. It facilitates a more profound comprehension of various subjects; in a more tangible perspective, this chakra endows individuals with an enhanced faculty of intuition. This has the potential to encompass a wide range of abilities, including detecting instances of corruption, perceiving incompetence in colleagues, discerning deception from others, and various other possibilities. The expansion of the third eye chakra heightens one's perception of spiritual realities while simultaneously influencing the physical realm in return.

When the third eye chakra is fully activated, it can potentially result in the experience of lucid dreaming or the acquisition of insights pertaining to alternate realms of existence. By employing the practice of meditation to activate this particular chakra, one can gain the ability to perceive alternate dimensions and subsequently assimilate this wisdom, ultimately fostering equilibrium within one's existence and propelling spiritual growth. It represents the pinnacle of perceptual awareness and transcendence.

This particular chakra is symbolized by the sacred 'om' symbol, which serves as a mantra utilized in both meditation and the daily practices of certain followers of Hinduism. This mantra is used to advance your spiritual knowledge and practices. The illustration also encompasses an inverted triangle and lotus petals, both emblematic of progression and illumination.

The seventh Chakra is known as the Sahasrara Chakra, which also refers to the crown chakra. Sahasrara derives its etymology from the Sanskrit language signifying 'a thousand.' This chakra, acknowledged as the crown chakra, derives its designation from its positioning atop the head. It includes the cerebral region, as well as the hypothalamic, pineal, and pituitary glands. The crown chakra also encompasses the nervous system, thereby conferring significant importance to mental well-being.

It could be asserted that the crown chakra serves as the body's ultimate conduit to the ethereal realm. The crown chakra is the chakra most closely associated with nirvana, or the breaking free of the ultimate cycle of life. It facilitates our connection with transcendental entities, while also enabling us to access an elevated state of mindfulness and cognizance.

The crown chakra is associated with the concept of self-liberation. The emancipation of the corporeal form from detrimental patterns, along with the emancipation of the intellect from pessimistic patterns of thought. This particular chakra is responsible for the cultivation of spiritual awareness and enabling individuals to transcend into elevated realms of consciousness.

Individuals who possess an unblocked crown chakra have the capacity to liberate themselves from unfavorable connections and possess the ability to perceive the authentic divine essence in everyday circumstances. They possess acknowledgment for intangible entities such as chakras, the universe, and the profound effects of meditation. An unobstructed crown chakra facilitates a state of profound spiritual tranquility.

The presence of an unobstructed crown chakra fosters the capacity to embody emotions of tranquility, serenity, and mindfulness even amidst challenging circumstances, thereby enabling one to maintain composure in the midst of adversity. Furthermore, it fosters a heightened consciousness of and reverence for the natural world and fellow individuals, thereby engendering a sense of interconnectedness.

The crown chakra is depicted as a lotus blossom with a thousand petals. One thousand petals serve as a symbol of the intricate tapestry woven by our existence and the continuous transformations we experience throughout our life journeys. It could potentially symbolize the immensity of the cosmos and the pinnacle of wisdom. These explanations provide a fundamental introduction to the energetic chakras. These pages lack the capacity to fully encompass the profound depth and significance inherent in these aspects of the spiritual body. In pursuit of the objectives outlined in this manuscript, we shall delve into the techniques and practices involved in materializing the advantages derived from a harmonious and unobstructed network of chakras within the tangible domain we currently reside in.

What is the function of essential oils in plant organisms?

The comprehension of essential oils in the realm of plant biology remains elusive. Nevertheless, scientific studies have revealed that flowering plants employ essential oils in order to lure pollinators. By means of natural selection, plants have acquired the ability to adapt and attract the pollinators they desire most.

The application of essential oils on the roots, leaves, and wood has demonstrated deterrent effects on pests, parasites, and herbivores, thus preventing them from consuming the plant. These measures hold particular significance as they serve to safeguard a plant from potential infestation and infection subsequent to sustaining an injury. Essential oils have been utilized in the production of insect repellents and pesticides, as well as fragrance, beauty products, and naturally, therapeutic blends of essential oils, owing to their distinctive characteristics.

Within the botanical structure, what specific components harbor essential oils?

"The frequent regions for extraction of essential oils are:

1) Leaves derived from bergamot, eucalyptus, patchouli, spearmint, and various other aromatic foliage.

2) Plant species such as ginger and angelica possess root structures.

3) Seeds derived from cardamom, coffee, cumin, nutmeg, fennel, and similar varieties.

4) Pericarp of citrus fruits such as lime, orange, tangerine, and even more uncommon yuzu fruits.

5) Moss varieties like oakmoss possess essential oils.

6) Cinnamon and cassia barks are widely acknowledged for their potent aroma.

This list is non-exhaustive. Additionally, raw materials extracted to obtain essential oils encompass an extensive array of elements, including twigs, berries, and tree gum derived from more than 400 different plant species. A solitary botanical specimen is also capable of producing essential oils derived from various sections of the plant.

The oils make a minimal contribution to the process of photosynthesis, and certain scholars have taken the position of categorizing them as byproducts of biosynthesis. It is imperative to dilute essential oils before they are applied to the skin; however, they can be inhaled without dilution through steam or by utilizing diffusing techniques or personal inhalers. To ensure proper dilution of an essential oil, it is advisable to determine the appropriate quantity of carrier oil and subsequently calculate the exact number of essential oil drops required. Please bear in mind that these measurements pertain to the overall quantity of essential oil utilized, as opposed to individual quantities, which would result in a significantly higher dilution ratio. Therefore, in the event that you are combining three oils and the dilution rate specifies 6 drops, it is important to clarify that this quantity refers to a cumulative total of all three oils, and not individually for each oil.

Dilution Ratios

Children between the ages of 6 and 24 months: Use a 0.5% dilution, which translates to adding 1 drop of essential oil for every 2 teaspoons of carrier oil.

For the application on the faces of adults, pregnant individuals, or elderly individuals, it is recommended to dilute the essential oil at a concentration of 1 percent. This can be achieved by adding 3 drops of essential oil per 2 teaspoons of carrier oil.

The recommended adult ratio for daily use is a 2 percent dilution, which translates to adding 6 drops of essential oil per 2 teaspoons of carrier oil.

The recommended adult proportion for Short Term use involves a 3 percent dilution, which equates to 9 drops of essential oil for every 2 teaspoons of carrier oil.

Therapeutic usage for adults – a 5 percent concentration – or 15 drops of essential oil in every 2 teaspoons of carrier oil.

Prior to administering to children under the age of two or individuals with chronic conditions, it is imperative to seek guidance from a certified aromatherapist or medical professional. Certain oils, such as Cinnamon and Clove, exhibit a significant intensity and thus require careful dilution, typically to a maximum concentration of 0.5%. It is imperative to conduct a patch test prior to using an essential oil for the initial time, wherein a diluted drop should be applied on the inner side of the elbow. The resulting reactions should be carefully observed over a period of 24 hours. The most prevalent adverse reaction observed is skin irritations.

Characteristics of the Third Eye Chakra" or "Overview of the Third Eye Chakra
Position: The Third Eye Chakra is situated precisely at the midpoint of the forehead, positioned between the eyebrows.
Chromatic attribute: It is intricately linked to the hue known as indigo.
Sangkrit: Ajna is the appellation assigned to it within the realm of Sangkrit.
The fundamental underpinning of this Chakra is consciousness. It resembles the process of developing awareness towards aspects of oneself or others that had previously gone unnoticed. Furthermore, it is conducive to the cultivation of wisdom, heightened discernment, profound spiritual

consciousness, and intuitive understanding.

Yoga Asana and Affirmation: The asana associated with the Third Eye Chakra in yoga is the downward-facing dog posture. For the specified posture, elevate your middle finger and bring it into contact with the opposing surface, while maintaining a slight curvature at the initial joint. Subsequently, position both fingers centrally in front of your lower chest. Recommended fragrances include the scent of rosemary, sandalwood, frankincense, and patchouli. The crystalline variety that amplifies and assists in channeling the energetic vibrations of the Third Eye chakra includes Celestite or Lapis Lazuli crystals.

In order to restore equilibrium to this Chakra, it is imperative to rid your mind of negative thoughts. Indications of a well-functioning Third Eye encompass the capacity to perceive beyond the realm of the material world, encompassing an ability to not merely assess superficial appearances, but also delve into the underlying dimensions. Furthermore, one's ability to handle their thoughts, intuition, and mindset is of equal significance.

Indications of a blocked Third Eye are characterized by impaired discernment, an inability to regulate one's imagination, distortions in perception, and a propensity for superficial observations. It appears that you possess a limited capacity to assess individuals beyond their outward appearance.

Conversely, an excessive activation of the Third Eye Chakra can manifest as a propensity for experiencing unsettling dreams, delusions, apparitions, and various perceptual phenomena.

Engaging in certain practices can facilitate the enhancement and maintenance of the Third Eye Chakra's optimal health and equilibrium. Document your aspirations in a journal or make an earnest effort to retain them in your memory. One alternative suggestion would be to consider embarking on a leisurely stroll during a time when the nocturnal firmament is adorned with an abundance of celestial luminaries. Engaging in this activity may facilitate the assimilation of starlight, thereby fostering enhanced consciousness and aiding in the activation of the Third Eye Chakra.

The Throat Chakra

Similar to the remaining chakras, the Throat Chakra embodies symbolism. Situated at the central point of the neck, this energetic focal point is influenced by two fundamental aspects: the act of conveying information and the act of manifesting oneself. Additionally, experts in the field of chakra hold the belief that it serves as a connecting link, establishing a connection between the lower chakras and the upper region of the body, commonly known as the head. For those who may be curious about the governing factor of this chakra, it is worth noting that the element attributed to it is sound. Indeed, this is aptly justified as the voice box, which serves as the chief organ for communication, plays a pivotal role in this context.

While the primary site of this chakra is situated in the central region of the neck, it is of utmost significance to gain a comprehensive comprehension that its function extends vertically, horizontally, and diagonally. Hence, the physical linkage of the Throat Chakra extends to the pharyngeal region, mouth, tongue, jaw, and brachial plexus. Its impact also extends to the cervical region and upper extremities, in addition to the thyroid gland, the bodily organ responsible for the processing of energy. From an emotional and psychological standpoint, it pertains to inquiries regarding interpersonal communication methods. In what manner do you convey your thoughts and emotions? Do you have the capacity to express your concerns and uncertainties to others without any hindrances?

In addition to facilitating personal and social connections, it is important to note that this energy center, when in a state of equilibrium, enhances receptivity to psychic auditory stimuli. Due to its positioning between the cranial and cardiac regions, a properly functioning (unobstructed and harmonized) throat chakra is evidenced through proficient articulation and adept attentiveness. The Throat is intricately linked to the second chakra known as the Sacral, which is responsible for nurturing and expressing our innate creativity. When a state of harmonious alignment is achieved between these two, it can be assured that the full expression of your creative potential will be effectively facilitated.

The behavioral attributes of the Throat are as delineated below:

Gaining comprehension of our purpose/objectives/calling (in relation to the leader)
Our means to express our creativity
Our affiliation with the metaphysical domain
Both spoken and non-spoken forms of communication, directed towards both others and ourselves.
Our manner of communication, particularly in relation to veracity

The predominant hues of this energy center are blue turquoise and aquamarine blue.

The Third Eye Chakra

The Third Chakra serves as the focal point of our consciousness and ability to anticipate future events; it is fueled by not only receptiveness but also the power of our creative thoughts. If one were to consult various authorities, a term that would commonly be employed to characterize the Third Eye is omnipotent, given that it is governed by the "supreme element" - an amalgamation of all elements in their most pristine manifestations.

If there's something that most people get wrong, it is the location of the Third Eye; contrary to most illustrations available, it is not situated at the center of the forehead. The Third Eye Chakra is positioned in the intermediary space between the eyes, situated slightly above the point where the eyebrows converge, in close proximity to the bridge of the nose.

From a physiological standpoint, the Third Eye Chakra has a direct impact on our pineal gland, which regulates our circadian rhythm. The placement of the gland itself holds symbolic significance, as it is situated within the cerebral region that responds not only to light, but also to the ethereal or metaphysical domain. Maintaining an optimally functioning Third Eye facilitates the ability to perceive even when our physical eyes are shut, allowing us to not only acknowledge the tangible realm but also embrace the realm that lies beyond it. This energy center asks questions like: Do you trust your intuition? Are you capable of experiencing vivid and lucid dreams? Do you possess insights that extend beyond the realm of visual perception?

The ensuing are the behavioral attributes:

Insights
Wisdom
Perception
Intuition

Please be advised that the following information pertains to both the material and metaphysical dimensions.

Purple is the hue that is traditionally associated with this particular chakra.

The Crown Chakra

Finally, we have arrived at the pinnacle chakra: The Crown. Similar to how our mind serves as a means of communication with the outside world, the Crown likewise fulfills this role, albeit on a profound level. Motivated by awareness and within the realm of cosmic energy (as some may interpret it as the realm of cognition and space), this serves as the energy hub that enables our connection to the cosmos.

Upon examining any depiction accessible through online sources, one would observe that the positioning of the Crown is portrayed as being situated on the pinnacle of the head. However, in truth, it is positioned slightly above the head. That is the origin from which this entity coined its designation, namely, the Crown.

In terms of its physical manifestation, this energy center is intricately connected with the pituitary gland, which serves as the primary organ governing our growth and development. Additionally, it exerts an influence on both the pineal gland and the hypothalamus. The endocrine system is regulated by the combined efforts of the pituitary gland and the hypothalamus. Additionally, the Crown exerts an influence on both the brain and the nervous system. This energy center poses inquiries related to consciousness or transcendence, such as: What are your sentiments towards a supreme entity with unlimited power? Do you experience a sense of unity or interconnectedness with the cosmos? Do you have a deep connection with spirituality?

To attain mental clarity, deepen one's wisdom, and cultivate an awareness of the transcendent, one must nurture the Crown aspect of oneself. The aforementioned are the behavioral attributes exhibited by this energy center.

Awareness
Consciousness

Connection to the cosmic, the metaphysical, and the transcendental forces.

This chakra is correlated with three colors: white, deep purple, and gold.

I am aware that assimilating these substantial amounts of information can be challenging, therefore I would recommend engaging in a thorough review and subsequently, diligently jotting down pertinent notes. In the subsequent chapter, we shall delve into an exploration of the indicators associated with properly functioning as well as compromised energy centers.

www.ingramcontent.com/pod-product-compliance
Lightning Source LLC
Chambersburg PA
CBHW050239120526
44590CB00016B/2150